Flame

Also by Decima Wraxall
Black Stockings, White Veil
Letters from a Digger
Going Home
Bloom
Stolen Fruit

Decima Wraxall
Flame

Flame
ISBN 978 1 76109 031 8
Copyright © text Decima Wraxall 2020
Cover painting: Melissa Wraxall

First published 2020 by
Ginninderra Press
PO Box 3461 Port Adelaide 5015 Australia
www.ginninderrapress.com.au

Contents

First Flight	9
Tattered	10
Flame	11
Feet Not Inches	12
Fire Kisses Ice	14
Boy's Own Adventure	16
First Train Back	18
Rowing on the Avon	20
Doc Knows Best	21
Storm	22
Campfires	23
Transcendence	24
Agenda	25
Edinburgh	27
Warning	28
Jagged	29
The Rattle	30
After He Died	31
Blickling Hall	32
Gleaming	33
Buddha Trembles	34
Blazer of a Day	35
Exalted	36
Pallid	37
Asleep on a Plane	38
Raw	40
De Luxe	41
Helen	42
One Tiny Sun	43
Huddle	45

Dollar	47
Facade	48
Black and White Ploy	49
Flying Jellyfish	50
Secret Garden	51
Glamis Castle	52
Fariola	53
Stick Insect	54
Fluffy	55
Capture	56
Snowy	58
Mr Smart Arms	59
Millie	60
Corvid Guest	62
Another Life	63
Angel	64
Terry	65
Bristle	66
Raddled	67
Doubts	68
Nobody Home	70
Grizzled	71
Mountain	72
Dating Site	73
Golden Age	74
Headlands	75
Secrets	76
Official	78
Girl Without a Face	79
Medal	80
Odyssey	82
Eulogy	83

Prison	84
My Parents	85
Timber Mill	86
Pluck	87
Censure	88
Shot	90
All's Fine On Planet B	91
Oppie's Gadget	92
Peacock	93
Glow	94
Barbed Wire	95
Street Veteran	97
Soar	98
NT Two-day Wonders	99
Slaughter Highway	100
Troubled	102
Clean Coal	103
Furore	104
Stardust	105
Careless	106
Blood on the Poem	107
Polestar	109
The Price	110
Access Denied	111
Toxic	112
Sacred Rites	113
Your Beautiful Eyes	115
Fantasy	116
Collection	117
Dystopian	118
Boulder	119
Why Me?	120

Departures	121
Purple	122
Dreamtime	123
Rum for the Road	124
Monthly	126
Poor Me	127
Derelict	128
You Called?	129
Last Flight	130
Palette of Freeze	131
Stranger	132

First Flight

This small and cosy birthing room,
a cup without a handle. Woven of raffia
and grasses, with a touch of blue ribbon

for luck – to match my mottled eggs. It's lined
with the best down and wool. Cobwebs and moss
protect the outside. A pleasing mix of textures –

environmentally sound. I sit and wait. All a foetus
needs is warmth and the push of my beak. Days
Pass. My partner swoops into our gnarled tree.

He feeds me tasty titbits, tempting my palate.
A thin cheep below my breast, and I know
there's not long to wait. The first sharp beak

pecks through the lining membrane. We trill
the delight of new life. Three chicks crack
into the world. Pink, naked, eyes bulging –

beautiful! I discard the shells. Three beaks scissored
wide… Frantic, we fly back and forth, to supply
juicy insects, flown off our wings by their urgent cries.

Feathers sprout and our fledglings gain weight.
At last it's time for them to take flight. They
Hesitate, tiny wings vibrate, perilous moment.

One by one they take the plunge.
Flutter, swoop, awkward soar, into
the bright blue and green of first flight.

Tattered

the old cockerel is lice-ridden
    and fading away
        into the husk of pastness

a pristine bird flaps his wings
fresh and red as the wattles
on his head   soon he'll crow

and strut the stage he watches
a barge at anchor in the bay
primed for action

    kids race and play on shifting sands
mums chat   dads ease corks…three…two…one…zero!

    bubbles rise   rooster animation
it's midnight – but something's amiss
people laugh about to kiss. Boom!
        the barge explodes in flames
      rockets fire every which way
    kids scream and stray   the cockerel nurses
a singed tail   in firework roar and crackle
        humans flee

at the turn of morn the new bird watches with scorn
      shakes singed plumage   leaps onto an Esky
        rasps a shaky cock a doodle do
            another New Year – of peace and goodwill

Flame

a voice yells into the blistering eye
of the sun   deceiver fibber fabricator
in the musky aroma of paint

each stroke changes dynamics
his brush drifts from the moment
into visions of lost dreams

the sun flares off vivid reds orange and blue
broken fragments ache away from two
figures searching unity on the canvas

lotus blooms and falling leaves
feel marvellously seductive and
mountains melt like snowdrops

yet a jilted lover sits *dans un* bar
dazed and disbelieving, sipping
the best French champagne

Feet Not Inches

your foot kicks and wriggles it reaches your mouth
a case of great fascination there's nothing quite like
the taste of the big toe   feet float before your eyes

it's a puzzle are they part of you? in the gloom
of the womb you've sensed so many bits spun as you
pleased   turned with ease to suck your thumb is fun

but what's going on? You feel cramped
    squeezed   feeling queasy   thrust and almost crushed
whooshing outside your watery world   gasp of air   strange cry

it gives you such a fright   your eyes blink   an amazing burst
of light   another cry louder – can it be from you?
what to do but open your mouth and howl   the odd

feel of cloth on bare skin…hear nursery rhymes you know
the croon of her voice   a rush of exultation – you suckle
her nipple   knead the breast   warm milk flows

heavy with sleep your feet kick and wriggle
you discover the beauty and power of her smile –
and yours – one day your feet bring acclaim

your first tottering steps   you talk in scribble
new revelation   you can see over the table
and feet are your preferred means

of movement   stiff shoes   scratchy socks
your trudge to school   feet jump pace and run
skip home   walk walls   paddle in the cool glitter

of the summer creek   you test each slippery stone
of boyhood – but cicadas wind their watches so your
feet splash and frolic through the river of a long life

now treading beside a chain of shrinking
waterholes – in the totter and hesitation
of your twilight bunion years

Fire Kisses Ice

                        one sombre day the lady
slips her tethers and steams away   largest ship ever built
the crowd forgives her maiden voyage delays

they shout and cheer   a long scar on her flanks unremarked
except by eleven grim-faced firemen sworn to silence...
in bunker ten below they battle the blaze – hot coal gnaws

at the ship's hull men's muscles ripple sweat-wet hands grasp shovels
they fling glowing coal from bunker to grate   in the luxury of first class
ladies saunter in fine silk gowns and French lace   flirt with dukes and earls

and the band plays a Viennese waltz   the deadly dancer cackles in bunker ten
below unsuspected   beneath diamond-studded feet she leaps in the lust
of destruction   her anger had smouldered for weeks...

now heads of state dowagers and patricians of every stripe dine   sip
double malt and fine wine oblivious to flames that burn and grow –
only three days voyage to go and just enough coal to reach New York

the captain daren't risk loss of prestige by late arrival –
or running out of fuel   here a young man savours his
briny fun and there laughing lovers on the run

– her married – giggle and pat her schoolboy son...
iceberg warning she laughs *such a hoot*   glasses clink
champagne toasts a new life – the titanic prow

slices the swell at thirty knots   bulkhead ten red-hot
steel warps and buckles   the dancer leaps to number
eleven   firemen curse   just when you think it couldn't

get worse…thud shudder – what was that?
mountain of ice   waves of green foam surge moan
unsinkable they said   hugs prayers   avoid tears

lifeboats few   brittle bulkhead rips   water floods
and roars   fire kisses ice   the bridge dips under the waves
and the band plays on…

A recent SBS documentary revealed a deliberately concealed element in the loss of the *Titanic*: fire in bunker ten.

Boy's Own Adventure

i

at fourteen
mother takes me out of school mid-term
it's then i meet her friend
he's younger than my dad and it makes me sad
pater isn't with us – or there to say goodbye

biggest ship ever built her maiden voyage
all my chums will be sick with envy –
but mother swears me to silence
rips my news to shreds
the tatters sink in green froth while we sail away

torn between excitement and dismay
i shiver   can't wait to see new York
three days to go
              iceberg warning
mother says what a hoot toasts our new life in champagne

a mountain of ice shatters her plan
i wait to join a lifeboat   mother gives me a kiss
you take my place boy – i'll be next
she laughs brushing damp eyes – takes a pink feather from her hair
hands it to me for luck   the last time i see her...
and the band plays on

ii
>   seems only yesterday
that great lady plunged to her doom
in blighty my father greeted me pale and grim
it's back to school for you young man
never ever mention that ship again –
or dare to speak your mother's shame

i stroked her name on a long list
while grief burrowed and squirmed
underground   and her pink feather hid
in a drawer
the enormity of her loss has never left me
these fifty years…

First Train Back

hollows at his temples hands gnarled with age
dad sits and waits out the days   waits
for a long-delayed visit   i read him

the paper every day   his eyes see only
the headlines   distance vision clearer
his first daughter flies in

from New York dad knows liza's around
his eyes scan the nursing home door
will she be here today?

what can i say? my older sister
has social engagements by the score
thirty best friends gather and gossip at her side

at last liza appears   it's been years   great to see you dad
a peck on the cheek   she keeps glancing at her watch
gotta rush dad be back soon   he wakes and sleeps

can't eat   racking cough   she's off on a jaunt
travelling far away   i say sis won't
you stay? dad hoped to see you a bit more

that may be – but I've seen enough of him
dad's ashen and gaunt   his breath stops and starts
pulse thready   I've worked thirty years in aged care…

on the phone i say best if you take
the first train back   our dad's dying
liza sniffs huh! how would you know?

tears in my eyes i return to his side
he sighs is that you liza?
yes, dad, I'm here

Rowing on the Avon

our skiff noses into the current
sparklets drip gold   double thrum
of gauze wings   green dragonfly

quivers on a reed   rower leans forward
dips then feathers the oars   water splosh
neophyte cox controls our rudder

he pulls ropes left right avoiding
punts and canoes   winged bolt
of blue   a kingfisher speeds

to a chestnut tree   yellow wildflowers
fringe the bank   father ties the painter
family splash and swim while grandpa

rests against red velvet cushions
recalling boating days at Cambridge
we push off   oops i shout watch out –

near miss – avon ferry   tourists gawp
and gesture   i laugh breezing myself
near an undulating glass waterfall

while luscious pink lilies shimmer
in abstract jiggles of light   an indigo
butterfly takes flight from my hat

and in a secluded grove
shadowed by willows
lovers kiss and chuckle

Doc Knows Best

doc invites me to her room   anatomy posters
instruments of torture
not sick not well I sit and wait my turn

behind her door chesty cough silenced
by the air of decorum doc tells her secretary
to ring mr x   he'll cauterise that bleeding throat

pills shapes of peace and calm
dispensed with alacrity
whether you need them or not

temaz? hundred enough?
you need your sleep…
but it's my chest

cursory glance at my ears   say ahh ahh ahh
no check of temp or bp   no history
low-dose antibiotic   fluids   rest

interview is over before it began

Storm

his thunder shouts and grumbles
through walls crashes against doors
a daily storm of teenage frustration

he begs and pleads for screen time
apps and devices in hand from the first
sliver of light to the depths of night

what right had that archaic pair upstairs –
his parents – to constrain his electronic
connections? they despair at this gulper

of mind and time an arrogant stranger –
a boy yet to emerge from the chrysalis
of childhood yet tall as a man texting

to the beat of an alien generation
not for them the quiet courtesy
of 'Sir 'exchanges with his headmaster

toby convinced how little they know
smirks and wipes crumbs from his lips –
a stolen slice of quiche

Campfires

tell stories
some true others
a figment of some

fiery imagination   flames
seize tales from sailors
and whisper

of a one-day-old baby
already speaking
of Babylon

Transcendence

you're well into labour says sister
injection sting   i spin into some
abysmal blackness   voices distort

and echo   am I awake – or dreaming?
it's a struggle to decide
and I'm secretly afraid of failing

to push my child into the world
six am   brilliant glow   rasping cries
it's a girl   her eyes blink disbelief

perhaps puzzled by this strange dry place
fingers and toes intact   moment of transcendence
and joy   my very own daughter –

a miracle clasped in loving arms

Agenda

Erin's flown a long way to see her mum. Nell's shaking finger taps out letters. Words unfurl on tape, one by one. *Nice of you to come. Expensive.* She'd ruled kids, spouse and dogs with the cut of her tongue. Trapped now, in silence. A padded collar supports Nell's weak neck. Erin recalls ones the draught horses wore, back on the farm... Dad feeds her green puree. Erin thinks, how long has Mum eaten mush? Nobody told me. Cough. Splutter. Dad offers Nell golden pumpkin pulp. She takes half a spoonful, pushes it away. Violently shakes her grizzled head. She's refused the doctor's offer of a tube. Her eyes flash *I'd rather be...* Life's counted in weeks– if not days.

Nell beams at her elder son, Victor. Erin bites her lip. *Mum's never looked at me like that. And the way her glance lingers...* Memories sting with blazing eyes and childhood strappings. Twilight. The others have left. Erin scrawls a note: *I love you, Mum. I'll miss you terribly. Do you love me too?* Nell swallows, tears in her eyes. *I knitted love into that jolly rug with her name... How many times must I tell her? Trapped in my own body. Speechless. Stricken at the thought of what's to come. Death.* A word that shudders forth in whispers. Lurking in every dark corner of the ward. Biding its time.

Now my daughter sits there, sucking away every breath of air. Arriving early. Leaving late. Watching every move I make. Waiting... Erin tut-tuts. *Mum, that nightie has had it. Here's a new dress. Green. Your favourite colour.* Nell glares. Erin rambles on. *Look at the quality of this material...* Nell stamps her foot. Grabs her red machine. *NO.* Erin lets the dress drop. She sighs, *I can't take this any more...*

Next day. A visitor brings white cyclamen, in green sphagnum moss. Light springs to the faded blue of Nell's eyes. Meryl's bright voice reads out Nell's messages. They discuss gardens, a happiness of bulbs and flowers. It almost seems they are both talking. Later, Erin watches Nell's angelic smiles, for the nurses. Overwhelmed. *Why can't Mum be like that with me?* Erin takes her break before lunch, afraid to attempt feeds. *Suppose Mum choked? Died? I'd be responsible.* Dad visits. Nell snuggles in her husband's arms, weeping. It's the only time Erin's seen her mother cry. And why?

Edinburgh

The Royal Bank of Scotland brings us a mind-blowing cupola.
Pale blue with myriads of skylights, shaped like stars, decreasing
in size. It's aglow with brilliant light and gilt decorations.

Outside, we gaze at the old castle, perched on an
ancient volcano. Time to admire the city spread below,
and smile along the golden mile. Stepping down side

streets, we stop, delighted to stumble upon the writers'
museum, replete with relics of Robbie Burns – a favourite
son. His funeral cortège included politicians, princes and citizens

of every stripe. Two notable absentees: his wife and current
mistress. Both, it seemed, were busy, giving birth. Time for us
to ponder the worth of his famous red, red rose of love.

Warning

i'm asleep on the afternoon coach
speeding along the M4
heading for Heathrow
adrift in a dream
i don't make my plane
can't recall my country –
or my name

i'm still befuddled when a purple vest
urges me to hurry
i grab the last place on the shuttle
to terminal 4   the untidy beard
in the window seat less
than pleased to have me
invade his space

he ignores my struggle with the seat belt
takes tobacco from a white plastic pouch
marked *smoking kills*
rolls his own with studied
indifference
and licks the cigarette paper
edges with a forked tongue

Jagged

curved wall   yellow lilies
jagged violet peaks
reflected intersected
            in the golden glow
i close my eyes breathe in *one two three*
breathe out *four five*
exit anxiety   hello me

i am the mountain
        the mountain is me
battered by rain   buffeted
by wind   seared by sun
i am black wolf   i howl to the moon
above rocky ramparts
    echoes drum in my heart

i pad with crystal footsteps
stumble   fall   seek answers
eye peaks of wisdom
breathe in   breathe out
conquer mountains
exit anxiety
hello me

The Rattle

of our telephone but nobody's there
A whoosh of movement by your bed–
they say you never die alone

Your life ebbs away day by day
At first the loss of weight
seems a blessing

Then the flesh drops from bone
You're gaunt and thin   grown pale
guessing the fate which awaits

Some cry and bewail the injustice
of it all when their time has come
    You choose wise words

Encourage the young
Hand out your treasures
one by one

After He Died

my daughter and I whoosh down a slippery mountain
i'm covered in mud   puzzled   how she can still be
pristine   we stumble through a maze of thorns

and nettles trying to find the way back   push
through the jungle menaced by huge spiders
and serpents   at last finding a new track

but it occurs to me we've trodden this one before
her boyfriend's car pulls up   she shouts, *someone else
will fetch you* and hops in   a screech of tyres   she's off

lost among thick trees   I stand alone mouth agape
not so much as a goodbye for me   stumbling
into the tar-black night   will i survive to see
another long and gloomy day?

i'd welcome even a glow-worm to light my way

Blickling Hall

beware the old staircase
where the ghost of Anne Boleyn
carries her bloody head
and Henry VIII glares
from a wall

a breath shivers across the lake
and growing low to the ground
mighty grafted limbs of an old oak
screen Tudor children's secrets
      – did young Anne clamber here?

hang upside down?
play castles   cubby houses
and hide and seek?
a young girl fair of face
dark eyes darting mischief

in her euphoria
of joy and laughter
did she notice
shadows mottling
her supple neck?

Gleaming

the old man hobbles past a weeping willow inhales the
scent of wattle   his twilight pooch leading him on a walk
gardens taking golden sunbaths before dark   he muses his

years have drifted away like blow balls in the wind
shimmering images recall bright eyes silk gowns music and waltzing
a whoosh of feathered wings and youth was spent   gone the stamina

of eagles shadowed by the gleaming casket of his future
he muses old age is fragile uncertain yet carries no
fear of death   goes home   watches more bloodshed on the news

quaffs a glass of red   nibbles crackers with camembert
and meditates on the bleak knowledge of crows

Buddha Trembles

school crumbles
dust settles
boy rescued
crushed arms

please

save one hand
to hold my pen
I must learn
to write

Blazer of a Day

sere trees dance in the hot breeze
air con magic inside Heidi café
table for two snatches of symphony
and me with my earl grey tea

she sips flat white   we nibble lemon meringue pie
seems yesterday this woman was my
little girl   now her own daughter nineteen
and at her best

while i stalk god's waiting zone
hoping he doesn't notice me
or phone   i laugh recalling glory days

old age not even a shadow
on distant horizons

Exalted

forever living   forever dead?
soul without a name   is the spirit real?
your firefly light joins other sparkles

in that exalted state   ready to serve
or be served   some dare return to the human
form   a voice cries it's not your time

wait   yes wait   until the burden
of your heart has lifted
flesh and bone and blood

forgotten   it's almost intolerable
adopting another earthly
existence – but something stirs

and a baby cries

Pallid

a visitor rushes
from my patient's room
deathly pale   i can't go in there

i say, why ever not?
there's a dead woman…
mrs bay?

she's not dead – just pallid
sometimes i need
to look twice myself

Asleep on a Plane

i waken   blinking to see
that everyone – except me –
have their breakfast
i'm miffed at not being woken

the downside of travelling alone
my neighbour rings his bell
he's ignored   mine goes
unanswered too

what to do?

give 'em hell   hest attention
i repeatedly ring my bell –
hated patients to do that…
hostess upbraids me   misuse

of emergency signal   sorry
i stare her down   *my bell's
been ignored   need breakfast –
medication taken with food…*

she asks another lass to bring
my meal   i wait   seethe   wriggle
had the medication plea registered?
finally the first hostess brings food

lukewarm – but i'm glad to have it
then trapped and desperate
for a pee   please help me…
hostess lost in action

i put tray and dishes on the floor – dreadful
thing to do but must have the loo
before we land

Raw

I step from a barren place
Of grief and loss
Into a green and fertile land.
Gordon is back. Fit and strong.

Checked shirt   jeans
Smiling at me from his workshop.
                          Last time we met

at the hospice he was gaunt and thin.
He's spent months in hospital. I carry
a shroud of guilt. Why hadn't I known

he was alive? His eyes glow. *It's OK.*
But I know nothing can excuse my neglect
And what of the funeral service?

We share a laugh.
Wonder who was in that casket…

De Luxe

i

Strangers sit ready to breach the gate
waiting for their numbers to be called
while de luxe shop jewellery craves necks
of the rich and powerful
given priority boarding passes

ii

In cabins on high we huddle eat and sleep
packed arm to arm thigh to thigh
Not for us orchids and trinkets
showers roll-out beds
and French champagne

First class bask in the obsequious 'Sir or Madame'
a treat for those who crave
importance
They nibble succulent chicken breasts
tiny cherry soufflés flavoured with pecan
able to quaff the surfeit of fine wines
with abandon

iii

At the back of the plane
I abandon my plastic knife and fork
turn off my screen
take three pills quench the light
and sleep through the long long night
ready to embrace a jet-lag-free
destination

Helen

She arrived in a wheelchair.
A well-cut suit hung from her
gaunt frame. The fine bone

structure of her face held traces
of a youthful beauty, despite the
ravages of illness. She'd say,

*Don't feel sorry for me, nurse –
I've had a good life.* She gave
dresses from her designer wardrobe

to relatives and friends.
Her jokes and laughter
made the worst shift bearable. We stopped

to say hello – even when she wasn't on our list,
impressed by her calm acceptance. Helen
hated being *a trouble*, reluctant to request help.

Her profuse thanks for everything we did,
made us humble. Long after her predicted demise,
Helen hung on, given oxygen and pain relief.

But one morning after her sponge,
she talked non-stop, gasping for breath. She asked
me to hold up photos of her late husband.

An airman…lost in New Guinea. A gleam leapt
into her eyes. *See you soon, darling…* A son held
Helen's hand until she slipped away.

One Tiny Sun

our jet glides   cabin thrum   mellow
afternoon light   tinkle of laughter
red-gold dapples peaks and shoals

of meringue   we've been flying
five hours   battling headwinds
another five to go   partial sleep

before touchdown at Hong Kong
babies wail   change of planes
thirteen more hours   big

motor gleam   the glitter of one tiny sun
reflected on metal   final gesture
of a golden day   screens flicker

clouds dipped in misty grey
voices hum   i ponder images
in the purple shades of evening

sea of violet – or is it sky?
pages rustle   headwind quiver
we chase the last glimmer

of the dying day – banks of clouds
blanket-stitched to night   lovers whisper
hold hands   a child giggles   wingtip blinks

against blackness   white noise meditation
shudder   shake   captain's warning seat-belts
clack   screens flicker   shadowed cabin…

i'm woken by blinding light   tomato juice
scrambled egg   mango ice-cream –
breakfasted   buffed and becalmed

descent   await the landing – wheel clunk
terra firma thud   4.51 a.m. at destination
London Heathrow Airport

Huddle

My missus passes her precious cargo to me
stored in a smooth groove above my feet
Covered by cosy feathers
Thin tired and hungry she goes fishing
We'll meet again in spring until then
I'm alone with other dads

Bent like an old man in my
black-feathered dinner jacket
I shuffle in the Emperor huddle
beaks to backs long darkness
Blizzard shiver   snow clumps

on feathers   Icicles hang from beaks
We're constantly on the move
against the chill   seeking shelter
on the leeward side. At last
the unconquered sun creeps back
We crave its feeble rays

Crack   squeak   new beaks open wide
We dads have saved the first feed
lost weight   I long for my mate
She's back! Fat and keen
to nourish our chick
We dads go fishing

Mum feeds and feeds again on my return
Junior's doubled in size   He needs us both
to hunt   Time for him to stand on his own feet
Like many a lad he keeps creeping back to his mum
Her *coup de pied* splat!   He totters to other fledglings
Mum and I lurch away to hunt leaving our chicks alone

Dollar

not a leaf astray nor a pin   daffodils roses
and daisies fenced in this Scottish town
set off by rolling hills yet just minutes away

from staircase houses and hedges clipped
into obedience   a wild glen of mist and moss
with a turbulent mountain stream

unrestrained it races
joyous over rocks   surges between boulders

in this secret valley a delight of pink wildflowers
greet you but the twist and turn of narrow paths
remind us dollar was once known as dolour – or grief –

two streams – the burn of sorrow and the burn of care –
the surge of one melds with ripples of the other
within a narrow embrace of stone this Dollar Burn –

a stream at the centre of town – gurgles between rows
of flowering fruit trees   the hillside drops away
hundreds of feet to the white froth of burn far below

walk above   tread the worn stones
of mellow Castle Campbell
once visited by Mary Queen of Scots

Facade

Two heart attacks   He's ashamed of spidery
handwriting   can't find the will to write
friends' letters   His dream ?

To see his girls grow into women
Husband   lover   friend of thirty years
Snatched away in seconds

It's the dread she felt at dead of night
and pushed aside   His passing isn't
unexpected   Yet it's a shock

In the ache of reality she wonders can I ever
be happy again? But she smiles and keeps smiling
for the girls' sake   Her facade seems the right choice –

Until they need counselling for depression
and reality hits her on the freeway
tears streaming down her face

She'd faked coping all too well
But where was the space
to grieve?

Black and White Ploy

Today I watch a magpie
collapsed – or playing dead?
She lies in dust, wings extended,

eyes closed, motionless –
stalked by her grey fledgling
I wonder at her game –

a plan to give her chick a fright?
She repeats the ritual – twice
It's then I see her being harried

by mynas – acting as decoy, perhaps
she hopes to see them fly away
I had never seen such a ploy

before – and right within
the garden
near my front door

Flying Jellyfish

      roar of wind
giant eucalypts sway and tussle   clouds scowl
limbs creak   turncoat leaves shiver and in
the sudden shine onlookers glimpse a giant

flying jellyfish –
white plastic edged with elastic ballooned
by air   we point and giggle   see its struggle

trapped in overhead wires   unexpected
downpour   umbrellas jerk open whipped
inside out   we shiver under an awning

peak hour motors' roar   mist spins
from tyres   huge puddle splash! two
schoolboys drenched clenching mobile phones

Secret Garden

Deciduous trees flame around the yellow, two-storey house. A honeysuckle azalea exhales its delicious aroma. Oaks and elms stir beside drystone walls bedecked with moss. The whisper of olden days and other ways drifts in the garden. Family ghosts walk the stairs. You score a four-poster bed, tall as an elephant and solid. You need a chair to gain occupancy. Not so much a place to sleep as a world apart, in a room replete with books. They shine the light on poetry and prose. The doorpost marks not one childhood but two: father and son. Their lives run in parallel for forty years. The son gains now on the old man, passes him at over six feet. At seventeen soon to finish school. His father at the same age had already begun medical studies.

Glamis Castle

pronounced *glaams*   home of the Queen Mum –
as a child treasures and fine paintings adorn
every floor

grounds with huge beech trees and a fine herd
of Highland cows long hair and impressive
horns worth a lot of money
status symbols some say

but don't joke with the locals and call them
heeland coos they won't think it funny –
eyes bulging one man said, 'We're quite
educated up here you know

We call them Highland cows…'

Fariola

fariola's cosmic vision illuminates
obscure levels of being outside our planet
sparking glimpses of the universe
with evolved souls in spirit worlds
    extrinsic to our own

in the hush before dawn
the moon all radiance and peace
embroiders our dreams in gold thread
while fariola leads souls over that vast river
    we all must one day cross

the breeze ruffles still waters   lotus blooms
lift up purple and pink petals aglow
with welcome and pink willow roots
undulate the hope
    of new beginnings

Stick Insect

i find a surprise guest   outside my front door a creature
in disguise 19 centimetres long   body armour camouflage
mottled grey magnifying glass in hand i venture
too close   he shrinks away a rocking pendulum

and living stick he sways with every breeze
his twig-like legs are bent at tarsus feet
he clings to bricks with hooks and suction pads
i think wow! a unique specimen – only four legs

but my scientific miracle proves to be faulty
observation   i discern two more legs stretched out
behind like long twin tails anchored for stability
to his chosen spot   i glimpse his tiny bulge of head

and read that his antennae brings tactile information
they move in concordance with his gait especially
on night explorations two compound eyes are invisible
to me but it seems he can see   on each side he breathes

through spiracles his defence mechanism? he holds his breath in sacs
letting it go with a loud *phush* to frighten off a foe   my stick insect
boasts green blood – hemolymph flows through his body
and it's hard to believe this slim frame contains microscopic

versions of human organs   ganglia control muscles digestive
and circulatory systems gut and heart   as for his sex life they say
congress may last twenty-four hours but the thing that puzzles
me – what passions inspire his minute brain?

Fluffy

jumps from truck   a white
one-eyed dynamo he races ahead
yap yap pink tongue

pant   puppy grin   fluffy leaps
shoals of snow clank whirr roar
blur of white on white

he disappears   thud
silence
lost in the sorrow of red snow

Capture

Her Dragon Space Station
gives stunning views
of our earth, archipelagos
in deep blue to the turquoise
of shallow water over reefs,
with golden shafts of light.

She hangs overnight in a sleeping bag,
her dream to put more humans into orbit.
Set free she can't sit or stand, but floats.
It's hard to dress but she won't complain,
thinking of men on the Shackleton expedition,
fighting ice and snow, half starved…

Her socks present a major challenge
She pushes hard against the wall,
pulls legs towards chest. In this
confined place her optimism
inspires the team.

Cosmonauts speak Russian, astronauts
Italian French English – her German
interpreter improves the nuanced
communication. A fighter pilot is her
technical whiz. A spacecraft brings
food and oxygen. Fruit and vegetables

spoil quickly here. Monitored from earth,
the supply craft moves slowly to avoid collision.
It must capture the Dragon or abort. The ship edges
toward the docking port. The chief shares a calm glance.
She adjusts the robot arms in out, up down, left right –
grapple fixture ready, waiting…

Perfectly aligned. She pulls the trigger. Capture!
She shares a high five. But it takes time to pressurise
the space between vestibule and station.
A burnt, slightly metallic, smell
of cracker nights back on earth
teases her nostrils.

Snowy

leaves leap and shiver along the alpine way
a mountain drive from Perisher
over the Swampy Plains River   vistas

of the Snowy Mountain scheme amaze
and electrify   thousands of war-weary men
left far-off countries to join forty thousand

Aussie workers   hard hats   strong boots   bulldozers
roared   chains clanked   concrete flowed…
fifty three years endeavour – water from

man-made lakes piped down hills foam white
clean energy saving our planet millions
of tonnes of greenhouse gas each year

in June 2002 the last whistle blew
cheers   joyous faces   hats thrown in the air
cradle of our multicultural nation –

one of the seven wonders of the modern world

Mr Smart Arms

I'm a cephalopod   some call me an octopus
I'd hate to be human   imagine only having one brain –
Me I've nine and what could one do with just two
arms? My quicksilver body and mind are one complex

nervous system and five hundred million neurons rival
that of your pooch   multiple neurons move each
of my eight arms   My central brain and eyes roughly plot
a path while my arms crawl and feel at will   each sucker

touches and tastes their way to food   Two
of my three hearts pump blood to my gills
the third manages circulation – and my blue
blood makes me a true aristocrat of the deep

I'm the star of my laboratory. Keepers
I dislike   watch their distance – or I may
ruin their day with squirted jets of water
Doc and his two-arm helpers study ways

to replicate my infinite degrees of arm
movement for prosthetics. We octopi
can move an arm readily even after
the connection between it and our main

brain has been severed. Ouch! On a happier
note no doubt you've noticed I can
switch body colours to blend with the locale
this fools predators – and rival males. Cool, eh?

Millie

i

friend companion carer
we walked a long road
through the blue-gum forest

of life without vanity or deceit
you made me laugh
and cry   watched over me

in those long nights
and days that slipped
through my fingers like

grains of sand   each one
more precious than the last
now i stroke your creamy

hair   sit beside you
whisper loving words
lay my cheek against yours

while my heart aches
at your laboured breaths

ii

in the bright morning light
you sigh one tiny breath
and slip into the jasmine-

scented air across the river styx
to wait for me   not goodbye
dear friend   au revoir

Corvid Guest

      We exchange glances
over morning tea, Intelligent
brown eyes. And I'm surprised

to see your lids close
from both top and bottom.
You doze   grey tufts of down

ruffle on your chest. Awake your black-tipped
white beak bites the itch of hidden mites
and if you could speak, I'd ask your name.

I take a ten-minute break –
or is it twenty? Claws embrace
the porch rail, just out of arm's reach.

Afraid to move and cause fright, I delight
in your black and white company. On this golden day,
pale tail feathers fan, edged with black, wings

outspread, you fly high, swooping
into my jacaranda tree. I rejoice
over a shower of lilac bells.

Another Life

he dashes in   no time to waste
off to bible study   already late
one flick   computer woes solved

see mum it's easy
easy when you know
how about a cuppa

bye mum   sorry to rush
she gives him a hug
telegraph pole of hard muscle

good deeds and prickly face
lope   grin   wave
darkness gulps him whole

loving arms   my little boy –
another life

Angel

The Angel of the North flies high, atop
a burial mound. Huge silver wings unfurl,
in tribute, to the men who dug and died, in

darkness, below ground. Their legacy, miners'
chest. Clean coal fires killed thousands more.
Black smoke and dust, furled from chimneys,

and fine particles crept into cells of lungs.
But tithes were paid on every ton of coal retrieved
from deep tunnels and pits, under private land. Coal
funded grand country houses, made lords and ladies.

Grew meadows of wildflowers, beech and oak.
Redirected streams and trout. Made acres
of lakes, from the mire fountains leapt.
Waterfalls surged. Boulders piled, huge

rock features. Deer grazed behind stone.
Massive gates – awash with gilt or 25 carat.
But never the guilt of conspicuous consumption.
Vases in blue, Chinese porcelain, fine tapestries,

too. Red and gold coats of arms pay tribute
to knights on fine horses, and dogs with hooves.
Testament to the blood and misery of war.

Terry

don't be fooled by Terry's gentle façade –
her *little* brother now twice her size
confesses she had him scared as a kid

green comfort bags Woolies own are never far
from her side   sunglasses stored in one   the red case
cocooned in another   a third contains a notebook

voices tell her she has a plane to catch but she escapes
the thorns and brambles of paranoia and delusion
a soul forever in flight   thin speech trapped in her throat

in the still of night she spills the magic of burnished
poems bright with wonder and delight   Terry reads
her works to standing ovations and caresses a leonard

cohen CD inviting her to dance to the end of love…
joy dances with laughter at her sixtieth birthday
the first party of her life   her eyes beguile

too soon Terry's life reels   too soon a bell chimes last supper
too soon we wipe our eyes   sing praises   and in the fragrance
of lilies we make our last salutations offering tributes to her poetry

friendship and personality   our acclaim inspires one woman
to declare our eulogies the most sincere she's ever heard
longing to join our group of writers – and she doesn't even write

Terry's smile radiates from her photo in the glow of being   a candle
flame whispers her given name   Therese…a soul soars high
and petals fall one by one   drifting away on the evening tide

Bristle

In the golden glow,
shadowed by cypress and gum
they send smoke signals of grief

One of the mourners asks,
Didn't Tom live with an American girl?
Marry her so's she could stay

for the free education?
A beauty – perfect features.
Studied law with a friend.

When love sneaked in
she asked for a divorce
Tom gave in with a grin

Always kind and loving.
But his mother worried –
or have I got it wrong?

The breeze teases and gusts.
A crow takes flight.
Other mourners bristle.

Don't we all
worry about our kids?

Raddled

the chemist feigns a smile   when the two arrive he rushes
to fill their script   they hold hands oblivious that anything's
amiss   take turns on the scales as if weighing their options

the man grubby but neat   her trackies trail threads   right pants
leg rumpled to her knee the left sags below the ankle   one foot
sockless   brown stains mark her grey rump   bare midriff

blue thongs score grooves through puckered thighs
her troubled eyes huddle under a hoodie   thickets
of bleached hair adorn a raddled face   she takes

awkward steps   makes several attempts before
a chair affords ingress   sits at an angle   some
hidden obstacle leaning her body out of kilter

her voice trails into uneasy ravines of silence
ya know darl I used to enjoy living here –
before i died…

Doubts

My buzzer barps before the first glow of dawn. Three late shifts in a row.
I slip my aching feet into stockings, tie the laces in black leather. If these
Hall's nursing shoes could speak, they'd tell tales of doubts and exhaustion.

But I'm a nurse: I smile. My legs throb through sponges. Sister C, moth-eaten
lioness, serves breakfast, wizened and pale as her veil. White gloves to protect
from hot plates – shame there's a hole at every fingertip. Sister doesn't notice.

Nurses giggle. Sister gives three staccato dongs on the gong. Quavers for this
nurse or that. Sends juniors on messages all morning – so much for second-hourly
backs. Dr B yawns along at eleven. He works night and day. Our admission's BP low.

Doc can't find a good vein. Sweat beads his brow. He does a cut-down for the IV. Soiled tray.
I rush him another. His white trousers and top bleed red. Sister C totters by a patient's bed.
Brings a hard apple. *You must eat something.* The tonsillectomy case snaps. *The woman's*

a fool… I say sister means well. Fiancé killed in the war. I ache. It's over a week
since my break. Patients call me smiley through two more shifts. Days off – shoes,
stockings, uniform drop. Hot shower bliss. Asleep when my head greets the pillow.

Nobody Home

The gate trembles, scratchy with moss.
I drag it open, brushing off green-head ants.
A wombat has made his digs under the house.

And I glimpse the calling card of a mouse. On
the porch Dad's boots ache, bereft of feet.
A felt hat and oilskin coat sigh for mother's

passing by. The cold grate mourns crackle
and heat. It regrets the dance of leaping flame,
and laughter from a euchre game. The parlour

floor putrid with possum poo, smashed glass
and china. Musty books, spines chewed by rats.
Shapes of missing pictures ghost the walls.

The door of mother's robe hangs, ready to fall.
Quilts and pillows, vandalised by pests.
Forget any lingering hope of guests.

Musing on memories and loss,
echoes of children's laughter, frolic
with dust mites, on turgid air.

Grizzled

venerable Sisyphus loves his rock
always seeking to have it reach
the top before it trundles
right back down

aspirations gasping
for the skies he tries
and tries   up down
he moans   cries

almost at the point
of high exhilaration
the mountain top glitters
within sight   on this hot

and sweaty night his
peak of ecstasy
drops right back
down –

within a slipper's throw
of erotic delight

Mountain

A poet unlocks the door of her
rented room. Puts down her laptop
and gazes in awe – at a mountain

of a bed. The former owner
was a man who loved to climb.
She shivers in the chill air. How to reach

that plateau of patchwork quilt, pillows
and sheets? She dons strong boots, grabs
crampons. Ropes uncurl. Oxygen helps

in the thin air of an armchair. In the poetry
of placing her feet, she sweats, edges forward
fighting fear and the sheer about face –

of creation. At last she's at the top – but doesn't stop.
She rolls into the middle of the grassy steppes
of another night. A lighthouse on standby

for midnight excursions into the libraries
of her mind and reality. She flicks a switch
nigh blinded by the bright rays, reflected

back from the vertical dressing table lake.
Sharon Olds glows from library shelves. She
tells of her blooms of fire. But our poet dreams

the night away in the arms of Robert Gray,
drifting over the plains of books, words
and imagery. Guessing there's a poem

lurking there in a silent somewhere

Dating Site

Dapper men with silver beards,
close-cropped, and cheeky
grins, wide as sin,
go quickly.

Shopsoiled and seconds
wait longer. Experts say,
lower your standards
to find a match.

She's not that desperate –
yet.

Golden Age

     a young adult
tries on personalities desperate to make his way
through social situations

without falling flat on his face
flushing over stupid things he says and does
trapped on the raft of life

struggling to survive until it's time to leave
father a boozer refuses to own his actions
mother intermittent explosive disorder

she'd thrash him one minute –
be sickly sweet the next
what's wrong with the family?

is it his fault?
his parents consumed by their own needs
avoid whales in the room

life is a row of knitting
drop a stitch or two
but don't unravel

Headlands

i didn't see it coming
no barp of horn nor scream
of brakes   no prior warning

that a headland crumble
was on the way   quicksands
of doubt and uncertainty

made me sick to the stomach
unable to guess what was going on
until the abyss swallowed

me whole   a shaking mess
unable to eat or sleep
craving only quick oblivion

from the unbearable
agony
     of being

Secrets

A water jug. Red and yellow poppies.
Six glasses. Him and me, reflected in the glitter
Of a gift shop window. Sasha saying,
It's yours for Christmas…

Luminous glow on my ceiling, June snow,
fallen overnight. The leap of firelight
danced away the indoor chill. But not

for Sasha, my sister, Vivi, and me. Three
against the world, we rushed to embrace
the freeze. Sasha the only exciting male

for miles – I'd been in despair at fifteen.
The only girl my age without a boyfriend.
My teasing glances lured Sasha into a

secret world of taking chances. No lad,
he worked for my dad. Beguiled by his jokes
and mirth, we dodged handfuls of flying snow.

Giggling at our elder brother Victor, only
nineteen, and seriously out of fun. His glares
of disdain, were frozen into a windowpane.

Boots crunched and laughed to the roll of huge
snow-balls. Chilled hands moulded ours into an igloo
for two. The kiss of Sasha's voice. A perfect place

for us to spend the winter. My cheeks hot,
melting to his giddy game. First love flamed
into the paddocks of a summer separation.

Expected. But his promise kept. My water-set,
deflected. Sent to Dad and Mum. She puzzled,
Why's Sasha given us this? I could only shrug.

Official

Centrestink it's the Department
of Inhuman Services at your beck and call
ready to obfuscate obstruct and delay –

day by dreary day   Commonwealth Seniors
Health Care Card? Care? Don't expect
to find it there   Send documents A B

or C and they'll declare with glee 'not received –
send again'   Official documents demanded
by the score and still they're after more

Your income well below the cut off rate?
Still the demons prevaricate.
You can withdraw your claim

at any time…so they pester and delay
but come what may I'll fight on
determined

to gain my rights   that golden tick
on my online claim – and put an end
to their shameless game

Girl Without a Face

Yellow jumper. The sort every fiancée knitted
for their guy. His grin. When your dad said you were
in Sydney, I had to see you… The rumour of her winner's trophy
third finger, left hand, buffeted my exhilaration.

Yet his blue eyes had danced the night fantastic with mine,
years before her.
The long-awaited shiver of his embrace –
My dream, made reality.

Torment in his voice: You lived so far away,
and, to tell the truth,
I was afraid of your dad. I know it's silly,
but I was younger then… Never had kisses

Tasted sweeter. Never had I so craved
to float away
with the running tide. But Nice Girls Didn't.
Not shadowed by a girl without a face.

Medal

Two boys whoop with joy. Boogie-board adventure,
flooded park. A stormwater surge gulps one lad whole.
In the drain his screams and yells grow fainter.

His friend sprints for help. Police, ambulance sirens.
Urgent council consult, trace the line. There's a slim chance…
A cop readies at a manhole, thin rope around his waist better

than nothing. The lad's wail knifes his gut   he's never heard
such terror before. Uniformed mastery chokes back his own fear –
one big boot then another, down a creaking ladder,

pitch-black roar and surge of water. Dim beams, six pipes –
but which one holds the lad? His screams shiver and echo,
almost drowned by the tumult. The cop slips, gasping for air.

Prayers resonate against his skull. He checks the first pipe.
A second, each is shoulder wide. A third, which one? That
frantic wail is almost muffled by the din. He figures the kid's

trapped against debris. At any moment, it could weaken
and a wall of water sweep them both away. Second by
second death steps closer – closer than a gasp of air. Let it

be this pipe, number four. Pallid beams slash the gloom. A
face gleams. Wet. Frozen. White. Let go, lad – let go. I'm here to
catch you. Float towards the light. He grabs the kid. *Say*

thank you God – and he isn't even a believer. The boy grips
him till it hurts. They emerge drenched. Hair plastered to
their brows. Blinking in the flashes of light. On evening TV,

they weep in each other's arms. Months down the track, a
rescuer's bravery medal. Broad smiles for the press cameras.
Hiding the pain of flashbacks nightmares and PTSD.

Odyssey

a broad arrow points me upstairs   lift transparent
everything else on the third floor hides in murk
low-wattage lights do nothing to ease my plight

rather than relaxing before my flight I'm frustrated
and disgusted by my moment of inattention   i search
in vain for the missing site   long gloomy corridors

locked doors   nobody to ask   I'd have thought the way
would be illuminated with signs   travellers lack time
for an odyssey like this   at last I pound on a door

a confederacy of office workers indicate the way they say
continue right on   at the end turn left   I find a woman confined
behind a desk designated human services   I crick my neck

bending to access a rectangle in the glass explain my mission
she notes my loss but i fear the likelihood of any return of my lost
property here – short navy jacket with gold buttons   red ceramic

brooch on the lapel – must be a million to one

Eulogy

Candles shadow and flicker. Hands shaking,
she stands at the lectern, wisps of grey,
cobwebbed against pale skin. In the aroma
of incense, her eulogy trembles with loss and love.

Folk whisper, wife number two – or was she three?
She cheered her ex at the Mardi Gras.
Cried with him over his latest split. Shared
an odyssey to China and Thailand. They
talked, laughed and danced pain away.

She admired photos of green terraced gardens
and red temples, tribute to his camera skills.
Outside, in the golden veil of evening,
tidy borders, marble memorials
and shrubs pruned to the bone,

she smokes   a raw farewell.

Prison

that long year of pain and doctors
the medical lamp glowing red   with relief
in the middle of aching days of despair

chiropractors   physiotherapists   pills
depression   anxiety   a long year
leg tingle   pain   pins and needles

thank God I can still walk – but
for how long?
from my bony skeletal prison i see

others limp   wrestle shopping baskets
and sticks   crippled in wheelchairs
pills beckon escape

but a child's clasping needs are greater
than my fear   hope glows
with morning   and fades

in the aching shrivel of afternoon
i crave only my bed
and the thaumaturge of sleep

My Parents

Nurses still recall
that tall, gentle man
my father

His equanimity the perfect foil
for my mother
her default position

rage
explosive, unrelenting
with righteous determination

to teach by rant
I try but it's not easy
to paint a rounded picture

of a volcano

Timber Mill

The owner wrings his hands. *Working alone, you'll never*
keep up with my mill.

Dad grins. We'll see.
No trunk can resist his finest axe.
The speed and strength,

of his muscled frame,
sees a large pile, growing
by the hour. Ready for milling.

The owner groans. *For pity's sake, mate,*
take a break. Timber mustn't dry out too much,
before it's sawn. You're the fastest axeman
I've ever seen. Thought of entering the Royal Easter Show?

Pluck

i gaze in shock at two grey feathered
shapes inside an abandoned bucket
storm-filled to the brim

lost to the deep…
had the fledgling perched on the rim?
glimpsed his image and plunged in?

struggling to escape those chill depths
heavy flap   sodden wings
whoosh

his mother swooped to save him
two yellow beaks scissored wide –
their last despairing cries

Censure

i

Mum straps my sister. Wicked,
for speaking out. I swallow rage. My silence
seen as goodness. It's my only weapon. When,

at last, the flow of molten lava ceases, mum
attempts to make amends. We say whatever
it takes, to escape the prison of her arms.

ii

Mum teaches proper English, insists on polite behaviour.
Cuts out dresses without pins. Patterns creep and wiggle.
She pedals, sings and sews.
The garments perfect attire – for clowns.

I make the mistake of joking to lift the gloom.
Mum says to my brother, *Laugh, Victor, laugh.*
He smirks. *I couldn't – I'd split my face.*
She simpers. *Of course not, son.*

I grit my teeth. Two more years…
In the crackle of flames, she reads us
Kazan the Wolf, pack leader in the frozen
north. He dies, snowed in by our grief.

iii

Vivi and i clean the house, wash, iron,
and fold linen. Mum rides home from cattle work.
She eyes the bare table, checks the clock.
Her boots rat a tat on the timber floor. *You useless pair,
I want my lunch on time.*

We've been busy, mum. Her barb, *You two
wouldn't know the meaning of the word.*
Beyond thorns and brambles, freedom shimmers.

At eighteen, I let fly with both barrels. Mum drops her knitting.
Leaving? Selfish… Nursing runs in families… Plenty of work here…
Her words batter like blowflies against the pane.
Tremble into tears.

Dad says, *Be her minder.* She's fit and forty.

Application, interviews, uniform measure.
Joy and heartache of my new career. Then it's my sister's turn.
Mum writes us letters every week –
until she can no longer grasp a pen.

Shot

i

fearing rape in an alley white
woman reports screams   she
greets cops in cotton pyjamas

shot by the man who answers
her call   friends inform her fiancé
he reels ashen *What? No! No…*

hugs loved ones and cries
for a long long time begging
the assailant have a heart man
tell us how   why?

gut-wrenching pain
planning a funeral
not a wedding

ii

a black man pulled over broken
tail-light shot
reaching for his ID

cop charged acquitted
in this repetition
of police violence

and cover-ups
people are afraid
to call 911

All's Fine On Planet B

there are no rules to tie my hands   it's all
go for my plans   chemical waste isn't worth
a mention   it wasn't my intention to make

rivers foam and stink   bodies float and never sink
smoking coal increases pollution   there's no bother
with a solution   as you can see all's fine on planet B

it's first in best slice of the yellowcake   i seize new land
when i can   there's no curbing the schemes of man   bulldozers
rip and roar   it's grab what i want and search for more

trees were the first to go   now i grow drug crops
by the score and still the addicts crave for more
best of all labour's free on Planet B   no unions

or crap like that   we keep 'em going with the lash
they groan toil and sweat – or crash   replace 'em fast
that's our way   my slaves trawl dead forests near a lake

nobody dares complain about what i take   great for me
– don't know or care about you   won my riches from excess
i don't give a turtle about the mess   black skies   smoggy air –
progress unstoppable   as you can see all's fine on Planet B

Oppie's Gadget

i'm ebullient bright   some say obsessive
teetering on emotional collapse
excellent physicist   pickled and smoked

war 1939–45 bloody undercurrents
i crave decisions   action   what's going on
with explosion? technology slow   complex

can't they understand the urgency? i leave
in a huff   work far into the nights   depressed
suppose the enemy find it first? we continue –

no other course   enormous project
technically sweet   i'll see it through
july 16th 1945 scientists war plant

will it work? one and a quarter hours
to go   tense darkness   orange
fireball reddens   pulses

rumble   shudder   champignon cloud soars
and far away from the Jemez mountains
some swear the sun rose twice that day

the words of Bhagavad Gita shimmer before me
i am become death   destroyer of worlds

some laugh   others cry
most are silent

Peacock

among the cumbrous attire
of winter drab   browns   greys
and black

this peacock joins the flock   purple
sombrero   pearl earrings   draped
cardigan royal blue   Peruvian scarf

striped tangerine red and yellow
green velvet slacks   claret bag
and mauve crocs

welcome rainbow man

Glow

Is it the green stillness nearby, or the glow
on soft foliage which makes me love it so?
And relish the long, trailing branches, with oak-shaped

leaves – the tree a giant now, bought as a seedling.
Large shrubs tell tales of long ago. They sway next to
my green garden room, refugees from the Himalayas.

A delight of red yellow and rosy pink blossoms. Grey-white
trunks recede into the layers of landscaped garden. Their solid
energy takes me back to planning and planting days.

Hands gloved against the sharp bones of stone I chose perfect ones
To nestle into dry walls. Brushing aside sticky bush flies, I laughed
with kookaburras. And liked to meditate here between growing

books and children. A magpie took flight, fanned tail white,
edged with black. I watched my son grow taller, pencilled-in
measurements compared to his father on a doorpost.

Wrote verdant poetry to explore my ideas of paradise
lush with the songs of thrush and wagtail dances. Skinks
ran from shoals of autumn leaves, awake after winter

Now my dreams and actions dwell in the sunshine of memory,
needled by pine. I pictured my next life, beyond human dimensions,
covered in nature's wallpaper, purple toadstools and moss.

Barbed Wire

in that grand house on the hill
pollies bury bureaucracy and tape
pulsing red with guilt and shame
        they spruik border protection
and mandatory indefinite detention

a shroud a shawl – it's all the same
for babies born with a number
not a name   birth listed as *incident – minor*

refugees rely on strangers
for luxuries – like kids' clothes
volunteers watch babies wriggle

to the rhythm of their mothers' voices
gurgles of excitement and joy ripple
from mother to child building

connections until a frown of guards
rattle keys   mothers and babies freeze
taken to quicksands of uncertainty

and fear   barbed wire rips apart   a year
two… mothers lose their smiles
can't meet their babies' gaze

fathers bring them to play
until one day they stop
obliged to stay awake all night

keeping wives safe from self-harm
infants lie silent and still
eyes dull   wrapped like mummies

one man raises suffering eyes
drowning would be better
than this

Street Veteran

the monster roars and claws
jaws rip crunch and tear
gobbling skeletal ribs   old tiles

asbestos and shattered glass
street veteran reduced to trash
nigh sated from his feast of bricks

the monster gobbles a side dish
of pine needles limbs   a trunk
and nebori   then it sighs rests

and sees that all is good
desolate streetscape
splintered dreams

Soar

A soft light uncoils all around us, an intoxication of white,
Beaches. Palm trees. And bare feet. There's a frisson of coral
underneath a pellucid lagoon. We move to the rhythms

of poetry, under the golden shine of wide skies. Rough-built
sailboats rock and splash. Laugh and chatter. Is this shining day
a dream or reality? Elfy speaks French with the *piroguier*

and I'm soaring on high to chansons of life and love.
My man urges, *Go on: take off your top.* Elfy shakes
her head but I let the teasing breeze lead me astray…

Defiant. Bare-breasted. Free. I stand at the prow. Relishing liberty.
Merveilleux.

NT Two-day Wonders

at the top end of this great south land
flooding rains transform empty watercourses
into rivers called two-day wonders

frogs croak hopping into the miracle of life
hidden underground three years
without moisture   fresh shoots   buds

and blossoms appear on wattle   witchetty
bush and mulga   aromatic grevillea   nectar
swarms with bees honeyeaters' beaks

dig deep   fairy wrens dart among purple cassias
rufous song larks gather twigs   refurbish old
nests and new with soft bedding   bird breeding

delayed by the drought   eggs cheep
and crack   chicks' scissored beaks squeak
for supper   lungfish aestivate until rain

they squirm and wriggle from mud
golden glints of light sparkle ripples
fish rise   gobble insects   dart and dive

the simmer of desert sun slows
the river flow   it shrinks to chains
of waterholes   fish a fine feast

for ibis and other waterbirds

Slaughter Highway

dawn departure
blur of grey   sudden leap from darkness
    thud   body scooped up by racing wheels

rattle clatter   we step out shaking
glad to be alive   huge roo felled – poor devil
    didn't have a chance

motor smoking   front buckled –
towed by NRMA   car a write-off
    we hire a 4x4   long drive   stagger to reception

motel full   we stifle yawns   quell consternation
hundreds of kilometre to reach the next…
    trapped into taking this late journey

plains curve into hillsides   fleeing emus dance
with elongated shadows   they dodge tangles
    of tussocks & saltbush   corralled against fences

we must keep talking   stay alive   admire the wide horizon
see the curve of our great earth   ache for pillowed
    oblivion   sunset skies ablaze   artist scumble

purple magenta & orange fades to black
clumps of mulga twitch in headlights   beware
    this night of goats nibbling grass at the verge

zigzag course   avoid humps of fur bone & the weight
of tails   slaughter-red mottles the bitumen   low-set shape
    lumbers into sight   i shout *look out!*

– sudden swerve   near miss   a wombat
what a fright – *it's his lucky night* – and ours
    broken motel sign swings from rusty chain

tossed sleep   tackle the road   in blinding
morning light a shock of undertaker collectives
    flock after flock   glossy black feathered black

wings flap   crows strut and squawk
stiletto beaks rip & tear   breakfast feast
    stripping each skeleton bare

Troubled

i

the steamy rainforest of the humid
amazon brings biodiversity in spades
it's the lungs of our troubled earth

cold currents off the Pacific coast drive
fogs from the Antarctic to the world's
most arid deserts   major rivers slice through

fertile valleys which grew maize in pre-
civilisation and large groups sailed woven
boats in three thousand BCE thriving

off the rich ocean catch

ii

the smoke of a huge conflagration
can be seen from space – our
precious amazon is ablaze

the clock of Climate Change
ticks more loudly day by day
pollution killing our fish

in dying rivers and polluted seas we looked to the
pristine amazon to help save our planet
from extinction – what or who

can save us now?

Clean Coal

Two-acre blocks lit by glitter
Lake Macquarie lures the unwary
the way we were conned is quite scary
hubby stopped to admire the view –
the perfect spot to retire, for you two…
Contracts and cash exchanged in a flash
The agent forgot the Power Station

We rue the day we strayed this way -
lock the doors, seal the windows
keep out pollution – nobody offers a solution
Black particles menace our home – my hubby
does nothing but cough and groan
Washed clothes hung indoors avoid the grits
The Power Station gives us the shits

Our lung problems get worse every day
for months they've never gone away
A toxic yellow – how I hate this haze –
close the blinds, avert my gaze
Pollies tell us embrace clean coal –
bio-renewables aren't their goal
But don't blame the Power Station

Emission problems need a mention
The EPA have good intentions – but
a million Aussies breathe toxic air –
coal companies and pollies don't care
I worry daily about our health –
coal kills daily and by stealth
Our PM insists it's good for our nation
He doesn't live near a Power Station

Furore

the edges of words are sharp today
imprisoned too long behind pursed
lips they knife their way between
the ribs of her homily   parsimony
shredded on the horns of outrage

notions of extra dollars from newies
tossed aside   exclusion drowned
by their roars   false masks
of forgetting ripped aside
fabulists laid bare *but it's*

not fair sniggered away blame
stripped from scapegoats
fraudsters' excuses overturned
disgust and disdain stain the floor
creep out the door   pour down

the stairs   bemused security hovers
when women of mature age
shout outrage   reject formality
to gambol in meadows of the mind
nurture imagination and originality

free to voice choices in coffee shops
exchange emails without penalty
on this day when members walk away
she cries foul   gives a great howl –
and runs away with the loot

Stardust

bronze age priests studied
the stars   mapped the heavens
inscribed a gold sky disc circa 1600 bce

buried and found in a forest
celtic rainbow dishes 2nd century bce
gleam still

ancient tribes live on in their craft
then and now stardust
a divine blessing

Careless

woman eyes a boy's red hair
spotty skin   *ugh – what horrible hands*
she says oblivious to his
sudden shame…those hands

drive tractors   push shovels   till spuds
fossick gold and emeralds   write stories
it's a lifelong struggle to make amends

in his old age a starched nurse
strokes his fingers saying
what lovely big hands

and a sculptor
casts one in bronze
for beauty's sake

Blood on the Poem

thick with clotted time
this poem promises greatness
sentence fragments
and bluster build walls
and barbed wire barriers

the poem is thin-skinned
narcissistic
finds scapegoats
for disaster in rants
and bombast

the poem spouts lies
and half-truths
to shore up its ego
and blames the media
for fake news spinning

in webs of delusion ambition
pulls toenails of friend and foe alike
it spews hate and unreason
in volcanic eruptions –
when not golfing

this poem cheers conflict
abuses creed and culture
makes circus swings between
folly and lunacy
small hands red and sticky

from wild west slaughter
of the young and black
grovelling to NRA donors
who profit from death
has this poem no shame?

Polestar

i

I had thought to reach this place of gnarled trees
and memories when i was old not with the sharp
light of life upon the grass and red robins on the wing

ii

small craft   huge seas   winds of unthinkable magnitude
argonaut   writer   friend   my hands grip the tiller
the wind sighs and settles and in this moonless night

a polestar guides the way to new horizons

The Price

patient at reception   just him me
and that darn waiting-room TV
near enough to see his cracked

feet broken sandals and grubby
trousers   i give thanks for a blocked
nose   he demands a note signed

off for overseas   *don't want to get
caught for drugs*   he's lumpy
confident   i picture some poor

soul sharing economy   glad
it's not me   then he winks
off to thailand special tour

a leer: *bit of fun if ya get me drift*
staff exchange glances
and in the silence

we weigh the price of poverty
for girls

Access Denied

huge distress denied access
to my grandson *if i can't*
hope what's the point?

yearning for that knock on the door
if I was wrong can't I be forgiven?
just pick up the phone and call home

didn't even know his name until last week
saw his photo on Facebook   i'm aching to
share secrets   show him the beauty

and magic of life   i'd cherish his heavy
innocence asleep in my arms   be joyful
over milestones   first tooth   steps   words...

grandparents   conspirators of love
help make the young all they can be

Toxic

After the documentary on SBS *Underground London* with Dr Alice Roberts

in the seventeenth century one child died
after another in the same family   this one
stillborn   another gone
before his first birthday   teething
blamed for his death

infectious diseases and rickets brought
weak twisted bones – lack of vitamin D
saw them easy prey   rooms of the day
filled with woodsmoke   killer chimneys
wide bottom   narrow top

air indoors dense and blue
coal the new fuel hailed
as a miracle   air less smoky
and seemed cleaner
but particles of carbon

smaller than a virus brought chronic
lung conditions   it killed more
people in a single year
than had been seen for
hundreds of years

lucky londoners the first english
people to face the wonders
of urban life

Sacred Rites

a disciple clad in white veiled hat   long sleeves
grandpa selects a hive   puffs his smoker
bee buzz calms   tingling excitement his
hand dives   grabs a frame of wax oozing
honey but it isn't funny when he stumbles

and takes a tumble   not even the yellow
scent – honeysuckle azalea – brings the old
chap awake   the doctor shakes his grizzled
head   closes grandpa's eyes   *heart attack*
no breath or pulse   his widow wails and sighs

but doctor he can't be dead – who'll
attend his hives? the undertaker shuts
the shiny lid and drives grandpa's
cosy casket away   friends and family
gather sharing tears and laughter

recall grandpa's loving ways   things
to ponder and warm their days
in the scent of lily and incense   the room
reels black with loss   his veiled widow
blots her swollen eyes   *i know*

there's nothing to bring him back
but ease my sorrow a little please –
retrieve the family necklace
the one he's wearing with a crest
of bees the undertaker lifts the lid

before he can collect the prize
hairs on his neck begin to rise   slight
movement of the expired chest –
the doctor can't believe his eyes
faint breath weak pulse   it's called

suspended animation – a first for me – the
widow wife swoons and hits the floor –
the doctor cries *move aside give her air*
grabs his phone   *operator it's urgent –
two for the ambulance…*

Your Beautiful Eyes

You put your family first, the years jogged by. School
days, sports days, parent meetings. And smiled at me
over a mask the morning my son was born
The first time I'd noticed your beautiful eyes

We lived through the daily grind of coffee and gourmet
tea. Your letters winged to me from Fiji, Turkey and New
Guinea. They throbbed with longing. *Wish you were here.*
And I yearned for one glance from your beautiful eyes

Craggy face, eagle's beak. When did your smile slip into a frown?
Indigestion, no time to seek advice – films to finish, battles to win
boss of busy department. Fined for driving at 150 in a 50 zone.
Dinner untouched. Breakfast ignored. Bracing for another hectic day.

At home you raged and yelled. A missing street directory.
Our son recording an oral French test. Your shouts didn't stop.
You refused to consider medical help. I put on the TV to record
Your favourite program. Somehow chose the wrong channel.

You screamed, *Why am I surrounded by idiots?*
Grabbed large scissors, blades pointed at my throat.
I'd never felt afraid of you – until then.
And couldn't recall your beautiful eyes.

Fantasy

episodes of family history, hidden in a drawer
fabrications of wonder and delight for my parents'
sake depicting life as a nurse a pollyanna fantasy

omitting witches who'd never smiled in their spinster lives
old-blood lips and nasty quips   I doubted we'd last
four weeks let alone four years   an escape of sorts

from mum's daily rants   my perfect preparation
for the tirades we faced in that wretched place
of early starts and late passes   it tickled me to find

yellowed pages of the year i topped my nurses'
group in pharmacology – 7th in the year –
I didn't realise my coup until the girls offered

congratulations   another letter carried my brother's
good wishes on the birth of my baby girl…and here
decades later she praises a new boyfriend – soon

to be her husband now my little girl
boasts a daughter of her own
Would I do it all again? Of course

Collection

He's a lonely old man   The visit won't take long   A crocodile
leers at tiny ducks in boots   A prancing horse makes to stamp
and whinny   A village drunk burps and clutches a post –

I'm not about to debate his odd tastes   Here a deer stands
frozen in fright   There a footballer leans in for a try –
and a clock croaks cuckoo – three times

But what's this?   A shrunken head?   Nervous giggle
Must be my glasses   Family statuettes leer   And a rusty fox
peers from a box   This *love to grandma* cushion is edged

in blood-red lace   That castle wriggles to escape its fate – or plate
A duo of silver candlesticks flame with life – and death   Triangles
of blue – magic symbols too   Horse brasses shine and a black

timber cross genuflects to the floor   A red and green parakeet
sits by the door   Though the bird's stuffed and behind glass
I swear it cackles *beware* when I pass   But why's he edging closer?

And what's that nasty smell?   Remember it well   tonsils op…
Yikes, chloroform! I scream   A mask drips   *There there my dear
just you lie down here*   The vice of his arms   My head reels

It's growing dark   Surely…someone…heard…me…scream?

Dystopian

i'm stunned to see that every creature
and everyone is under attack
our very civilisation is doomed

helpless to save myself – or others
i shudder   oh the piles of broken bodies
and spilling flesh   the sickly smell   eyes that burn

with bloodlust   how can such horror be real?
heavy with dread   dripping red i run
dodging gunfire and blade

should i stumble and fall ?
play dead
hide in plain sight?

sudden rescue   bright rays of morning light
all atremble i blink relief
weak from that dank and dismal night

Boulder

i

husband   lover   friend   boulder
in the landscape of our family
stricken

in his prime   fading from sunlight
into night   his grey eyes seek mine
raw with adoration

we kiss on the lips one last time
summer grasses sway and undulate
driven by the scythe of time

ii

he climbed up and up into rocky
ramparts – unable to follow
i swayed below clinging

to the tree of life the day we died

Why Me?

i scream to the moon   curse the pitiless sun
lie weeping in the grass under an apple tree
why me?   my voice   my identity ALS happens

to others…not me   the old   the weak   the lame
me – strong and healthy   no drink or drugs
hard work   horses   the farm   far from the

constipated complicated evils of the city
my voice slashed at kids   coaxed dogs from
hidden places   cut egocentric husbands

down to size   saw the truth in frightened eyes
railed against follies and television   thrilled to
miracles and mountains   a thief invaded my safe

clean home   leaving me angry   afraid
alone   shivering on the edge of disaster
lost in a vortex of sounds and voices   ready

to explode with frustration   god where's it gone
my communication?   i long to sing and shout
and be   it's not me tottering to the loo choking

on mush   but under frost-clear skies of eternity
a thought stumbles in –
why not me?

Departures

A coterie of passengers wait palpate screens black and brown suits
Ripped jeans floral dresses and a skirt cut off just below the bum

Toddlers grizzle for treats   kids wriggle in their seats
Teens buried in devices   a frown of mums scold

Rubber wheels tsk tsk tsk on marble
A people mover delivers its cargo

To gate number ten   the bored driver sighs
Backs up   warning bells jingle   one load

Adds to another   white-haired or bald
Wobbly and frail knobbled hands clutch

Walking sticks boarding passes and passports
Ageless adventurers – about to fly

Purple

Ted said he and Vera had endured
the gamut of dull wives over the years.
Fearing Gordon's would be the same.

They expected some gum-chewing housewife,
who discussed the price of soap over lunch.
Gobsmacked to see me arrive. Ted said,
Tall and stately. Vera added, *and that purple
gown ruffled at the hem. Wide belt, cinched into
your slim waist. Embroidered with purple, yellow*

*and orange flowers. You could have stepped from the pages
of Vogue.* We dined on trout sweet and moist, with almonds.
Enjoyed a side of potato slices, baked in cream

Savoured an aromatic dry white. Drooled
over strawberries with crème caramel.
Conversed over wonders of the Renaissance,
Art and poetry. Travelled to Istanbul
and London, with a side trip to
Carcassonne on the way

Dreamtime

Sisters three nubile and free – the old story
their forbidden love causes a scandal
and they're transmuted forever

into blocks of stone   three lads of the rival tribe
unpunished   the sisters gaze at the veil of gold
draped over the Megalong and Jamieson valleys

marvel at the splendid vista of Mount Solitary
its granite face gazes back and chats wistfully
of the Ruined Castle resplendent in purple

Rum for the Road

i

Old mates, three-day binge. Mum must wonder
where the hell we are. If only there was a phone…
Glasses clink, a toast or three. *Rum for the road.*

Downed at a gulp. Daddy grabs his keys, sways –
buffeted by booze. *Let's go, girls. Mustn't worry
your mother.* The wife of dad's pickled mate shares

a worried glance. *Wait, Joly, dry out…* His scornful laugh.
Never felt better. At twelve I shiver. *No, I'll not go – you're
drunk.* His bleary eyes struggle to focus. *Come or I'll drive off*

and kill myself. High in the cabin, I can hardly breathe.
I'm not ready to die. Vivi clutches my arm. I pat my kid sister.
Big hands clutch the wheel – our lorry misses the gatepost

by inches. Judders along the road. The engine speeds up.
Slows down. Where are the cops when you need them?
My feet press hard against the floor. Lurch. Kangaroo hops.

I talk on and on, just to keep Dad awake. Hairpin bends.
Valleys far below. Dreading each narrow cutting and steep
incline. Wheels caress the edge. Here a truck overturned.

A father killed. His son walked miles in darkness for help.
Careful, Daddy, careful. He chortles. *Say your prayers
girls, say your prayers. Only sixty miles to go…*

ii

Mum meets us at the homestead gate. Puce with rage.
*How dare you put our girls through such an ordeal –
driving in your state.* Dad bears her tirade in silence.

Falls asleep in his clothes. I make to share my
pain. Mum turns on me like a viper. *It's none
of your damned business.* I swallow rage.

And Vivi shakes her knowing head.

Monthly

Last period – I won't miss the gut
pains, cramps, and stained underwear.
Better than the alternative – but like a
crotchety aunt arriving without invitation,

it was only welcome long ago. Oh, that first
burst of excitement, my sense of achievement
over being a woman. The thrill at joining the ranks

of Marilyn Monroe, Sophia Loren,
and Grace Kelly. Secretly, I'm glad that part
of my life is over. The idea of a third child

was long rejected. But I'm surprised to find,
at the back of my mind, pangs of loss. Even
twinges of regret at the shrinking choices.

Poor Me

We haven't spoken for some time and my emails
bounced back   I'm keen to catch up   On return from the UK
I ring her saying I've just returned… Without missing a beat

she launches into a long oration   *I've no need
to go away   I'm happy to potter in my garden
all day*   I laugh and say *so glad we've cleared that*

*up – who'd want to visit the Great Marble Mosque
in Abu Dhabi? Decorated with belle de jour? Or wander
around the halls of the new Louvre? Gazing at the*

*marvellous cupola dappled with stars of summer
sunlight? Or sip cakes and champagne in the Royal
Palace Hotel? I know it's all a pain but then again –*

Somebody's got to do it   Poor me

Derelict

Student accommodation. A rough figure
sprawls against the warehouse door.
Bottle in brown-paper bag clutched to his chest.

Her entry's blocked. Weary. Shopping-laden arms…
She ponders how to get past. Acts tough.
C'mon there, move on. Out of my way.

Red-faced he totters to his feet. A shaky bow. He
sweeps a battered fedora from his balding pate.
Whiskered wrinkles, toothless grin.

Yes, ma'am. He backs away. *Whatever you say, ma'am.*
Inside, she leans into the closed door.
Whew! That was easy.

His scream almost splinters the weathered timbers.
Miserable sow! Bitch! Rotten old cow.

You Called?

I cling to the handpiece with arthritic fingers.
Thrust onto this buckjump ride, this
diatribe, this stream of consciousness

ramble. Galloping through the endless thorns
and thickets of her life, I lose all sense of reality.
Who are these people? Puppets she pulls

in and out of view – aunts, uncles, a friend
or two. Her dead husband joins the party.
An hour's jaw-dropping journey

of indulgence. This one-woman show,
this soliloquy of things past. Deaths, births,
old scores… She pays scant attention

to my scattered words, wedged between
hers, my feeble attempts to transform
her monologue, into conversation.

Last Flight

the pale wonder of open sky
wisped with blurs of white
backdrop to an evening parade

squadron of seagulls pinions outspread
silver-edged white in the dying light
they float on thermals   circle   wobble   adjust

random dives   some rise   the birds intermingle
soar but never touch   choreographed exuberance
on this last flight shadowed by wings of night

far from their daily fun   swooping
above mellow streets to drop excess
cargo on unwary human heads

Palette of Freeze

I meditate on the palette of freeze. Sedge, toad rush
and grasses, furred white with hoar. The crunch
of verglas crackles underfoot. My boots lead

onwards to the shine of a glass. In the chill
afternoon air, ripples are stilled. I stop at the
edge of darkness, savouring the last rays

of the dying day. It's the mathematics of winter
and life, rendered in ice. Triangles, large and small,
pave the surface. Lines connect, intersect and overlap

memories rendered in gold. Does blue mark the great
unknown? See the shapes and veins of leaves. The way
thick lines hold conferences with thin? I savour the vista

in an ecstasy of wonder and delight, until the whoosh
and scream of plovers makes me laugh – in fright

Stranger

smoke twirled from a chimney far from the rutted road
beside a track fragrant with wattle and eucalypt
the woman stood outside her cabin door   a stranger
tied up his mare the broken gate squeaked open

she made him tea – as you did in pioneer days
he gobbled damper and home-made cake
downed two or three mugs of tea smacking

his thick lips   she shivered at the way he eyed
her curves…her husband away droving –
and not expected home for weeks – forest

giants gulped the dying rays of the day
every glance from this outsider triggered
alarm   her kids stepped out of reach

how could she make him leave? she hid
the tremor of her hands under her pinny
forced a smile   *you must excuse me*

she said   *my hubby's due home for tea –
he'll be cross if it's late*   the stranger paled
his stained hat sprang to his head

the gate creaked   his grey galloped him away
swallowed by twilight she hugged the little
ones   wiped her eyes   made their tea

the shotgun lay awake beside her
through that long and sleepless
night – inches from her reach

www.ingramcontent.com/pod-product-compliance
Lightning Source LLC
Chambersburg PA
CBHW070916080526
44589CB00013B/1315